Victorian Domestic Abuse

Carol Ann Lewis

DEDICATION

To all the Victorian women who fought for change and gave us the freedom we enjoy today

ORIGINS

Where did it all begin? Who decided that one half of society had to be subjugated by the other half and whose idea was it to punish that other half if it dared to step out of line? Who decided women needed to be controlled and chastised? These are questions we will probably never have the answers to, we weren't there to know for sure. In her book 'Women's History of the World', Rosalind Miles attributes it to the fall of goddess worship and the evolution of human thought. Ancient people believed all life began with woman, a magical act with men appearing to play no part, however with the realisation of cause and effect, man's part in reproduction became clear and he wasnt happy to be sidelined. The rise of the phallus led to the downfall of the Goddess. Miles goes on to say that in the millenia before the birth of Jesus, mythologies speak of the overthrow of the Mother Goddess, for example in Celtic folk myth where three wise crones meet the son of the War God in battle and after may clashes they are subdued and humbled before him.

The earliest reference to women being the property of men is in the Code of Ur Nammu, the King of Sumer, who composed a law code around 2047 – 1750 BCE. It stated that if a virgin slave woman of a man was raped, the perpetrator had to pay compensation to the man who owned her. Women could also be sold, divorced if unable to have children or drowned if refusing to have them. Similar laws existed in the 18th century BCE in the code of Babylonian King Hammurabi. The killing of a pregnant maid servant could be rectified with a monetary fine. The code also shows the double standards already in existence, men could have affairs with maid servants and slaves but a woman doing the same would be tied up and thrown into the nearest river, along with her lovers. The Roman code of Paterfamilias entitled a husband to kill his wife if she was found to be having an affair however if the situation was reversed she just had to put up with it. A Roman woman could also be left to another man in her husband's will. In Greece, women were confined to their homes and female babies could be abandoned to die, unless a passer by took pity on them.

With the growth of Christianity attitudes towards women became worse even though Jesus showed many acts of compassion towards them for example the stoning of Mary Magdalene. In the Bible women are told they must be quiet, not teach or have any authority over a man. They are also responsible for bringing sin in to the world, for it was only Eve that was deceived and not Adam. This is first introduced in Genesis, God tells Eve her only desire will be for her husband and he would rule over her. Also with Christianity emerged the notion that women are dirty from the beginning of their reproductive life until its end. A woman was unclean for seven days after giving birth to a son but if she gave birth to a daughter, as if in punishment for doing so she was unclean for fourteen days. To embrace a woman, according to Odo of Cluny was to embrace a sack of manure.

By contrast in medieval Wales, at birth there were no distinctions between males and females, until after baptism at which times males were worth the double of females. Men were still classed as superior however marriage was seen as more of a contract between both parties and the husband was not allowed to beat his wife at will. If he did find himself having to chastise he could deliver no more than three blows. The wife also had some rights. If her husband dishonoured her by committing adultery, he was to pay a fine and if he did this three times she could divorce him, retaining her property and her status. Under the traditional laws of Wales, though life was probably not perfect, it seems men and women enjoyed more equality than other areas of the world, until the time of the Norman invasion and the expansion of the English state that is, when Catholicism brought Canon Law which imposed marriage for life.

Canon Law encouraged the chastisement of unruly wives. Gratian, taught church law at the University of Bologna around the 12th century and compiled a law book, Decretum Gratiani. In it he includes such statements as

"woman is not called so because of the sex of her body but because of the weakness of her mind"

and

"a man may chastise his wife and beat her for her own correction, for she is of his household and therefore the lord may chastise his own .. so likewise the husband is bound to chastise his wife in moderation, unless he be a clerk in which case he may chastise her more severely"

and

"the husband is the head of his wife and the wife is the body of her husband so that a wife may make a vow of abstinence if her husband allows her to, but which she may not fulfill if her husband forbids her to"

In other words she has no right to say 'no'.

Friar Cherubino of Siena in the second half of the 15th century had this to say in his Rules of Marriage.

"When you see your wife commit an offence, dont rush at her with insults and violent blows ...scold her sharply, bully and terrify her. And if this still doesnt work, take up a stick and beat her soundly for it is better to punish the body and correct the soul ... Readily beat her, not in rage but out of charity for her soul so that the beating will rebound to your merit and her good"

Chastisement was usually carried out publicly using devices such as iron muzzles that pressed into the tongue. The Derbyshire Brank for example was attached to a woman's head, secured around her face and mouth and prevented her from speaking or eating.. A chain was also attached so she could be led around or secured to a spot. A wife could have her nose and ears severed for commtting adultery. In the ballad, 'A Caution for Scolds', published around 1685, the husband goes to a doctor whose cure for her scolding is to tie the wife to the bed, shave her head and cut out her tongue and let her bleed a gallon. Here we can see parallels with witch hunts, when a witch bled she lost power, when the wife bled she lost her ability to scold.

Husbands though, had to have a good reason to give chastisement and those who beat their wives just for the hell of it found they would also be punished. Ran Tan Tan, an old folk custom drew attention to a wife beater, or other troublesome persons in the community. An effigy of that person was made and carried around the village on a pole. Accompanying it would be a large crowd banging drums or kitchen utensils. The party would congregate at the accused's house for three nights then drown the effigy in the village pond. What effect this had, who knows, perhaps he would be so ashamed he would stop, or leave the village.

The chastisement of wives was reinforced in 1782 when an etching by caricaturist James Gilray was published. It shows Judge Buller carrying armfuls of sticks after reputedly ruling that a man had the right to correct his wife by beating her as long as the stick was no wider than his thumb. The law became known as the Rule of Thumb though some sources say it didn't actually exist as a law. Even if it didn't exist though, Judge Blackstone in his Treatise on English Common Law stated that a man could correct his wife

"for as he is to answer for her misbehaviour the law thought it reasonable to entrust him with this power of restraining her, by domestic chastisement in the same moderation that a man is allowed to correct his apprentices or children .. but this power of correction was confined within reasonable bounds as the husband was prohibited from using any violence towards his wife"

and

"The husband and wife are one, and that one is the husband"

Women, they were well aware of the inequality in society and they began to fight back. Mary Wollstonecraft was born in Spitalfields, London in 1759 to an abusive father. Her mother died in 1780 and she left home to pursue a career in writing. At the same time she worked as a translator and in 1784 established a school with her sister Eliza and best friend Fanny and wrote a pamphlet 'Thoughts on Education for Daughters'. In 1792 she met Captain Gilbert Imlay and American adventurer. She had a daughter with him but eventually he left her. She then met William Godwin and married when finding out she was pregnant. Her daughter, Mary (Shelley, of Frankenstein fame) was born in 1797 however ten days later, Mary Wollstonecraft died.

Her most famous work was published in 1792 'A Vindication of the Rights of Woman' and it addressed the disadvantages women had in society.

"I am scarcely able to govern my muscles when I see a man start with eager and serious solicitude to lift a handkerchief or shut a door when the lady could have done it herself had she only moved a pace or two"

"Men in their youth are prepared for professions and marriage is not considered as the grand feature in their lives whilst women, on the contrary have no other scheme to sharpen their faculties"

"Business of various kinds, they might likewise pursue if they were educated in a more orderly manner which might save many from common and legal prostitution"

"Would men but generously snap our chains and be content with rational fellowship instead of slavish obedience they would find us more observant daughters, more affectionate sisters, more faithful wives, more reasonable   mothers   —   in   a   word   better   citizens"

19TH CENTURY

The state of play for women at the beginning of the 19th century was that they had no choices in life whatsoever. They were the property of men, men controlled all the money, children and property. Girls received little education, their sole purpose being to marry and reproduce. A single woman attracted pity and disapproval. There were no jobs for women, except low paid ones and many professions were closed to women. Once married all their possessions and money belonged to the husband. Any wages she earned belonged to the husband. Her body was also his, she had no right to say no to sex or childbirth. The children were his too, if he decided he was going to hand them over to a mistress he could. If she escaped, or if he left her and she formed a new life, he could turn up at the door and take everything she had because she was still his wife. The only way to obtain a divorce was through a private Act of Parliament. It was only on the grounds of adultery though and for wives, only if life threatening cruelty was involved. It was also an expensive process which meant the majority of women couldnt afford it and so, this is what was happening behind closed doors in Victorian homes.

In May 1800, Mr Meadows of Kippis Hall near Pontefract suddenly called his wife's maid into the drawing room. He then threatened to stab her with his sword. His wife intervened and diverted his attention allowing the maid to leave the room but then he attacked his wife instead. He stabbed her three times and cut her throat with such ferocity that he almost severed her head. The servants were alerted when one of the children ran downstairs shouting "Pappa has killed Mamma". The servants sent for a party of the Pontefract Volunteers who discovered he was armed with three pistols as well as a sword. They secured him and marched him off to York Castle.

He probably faced trial and was hung.

In January 1810, William Stevens, a driver of the Hastings stage coach was charged with beating his wife and child. Mrs Stevens complained she had long been the victim of her husband and had been under the hands of the surgeon after the blows he had given her. One Friday he had beaten her and also their infant son, aged 7. He made him strip naked then he beat him with a horse whip until the child collapsed. He suffered a fracture to his head. Mrs Stevens's screams alerted her landlord and his wife. She then jumped out of the window. Landlady, Mrs Lovedon said she discovered the child bleeding and when seen by a surgeon he stated that he had seen fractures of less severity cause death. Mr Stevens declared it was all a lie, the child had fallen against a door. As for cruelty to his wife he said she appeared too friendly with the landlord for his liking, a claim that was denied. Mr Stevens was sent for trial.

In September 1812, Frances Evans was indicted for murder. He had beaten his wife violently on the head and had thrown her out of a window. Another count charged him with violently beating her, drawing a knife on her and threatening to murder her from which she became so frightened she jumped out of a window. She fell onto her left hip and elbow. She was carried to the London Hospital where she was kept for nine days. The surgeon said she had severe bruising to her face and head, her right jaw was fractured and also her left thigh.

Her autopsy showed a mass of inflammation on the brain. Mr Evans gave a long defence, he denied all charges and said his wife was of a bad character who he had been very kind towards. The jury found him, not guilty.

CAROLINE NORTON

Caroline was born in 1808. She was 16 when she met George Norton, M.P. for Guildford and by 1827 they were married. It wasn't long into their marriage, about two months when he attacked her for giving an opinion of her own.

"We had been married about two months, when one evening after we had all withdrawn to our apartments we were discussing some opinion Mr Norton had expressed. I said that I had never heard so silly or ridiculous a conclusion. This remark was punished by a sudden and violent kick, the blow reached my side, it caused great pain for several days and being afraid to remain with him I sat up the whole night in another apartment".

It didnt stop there, on another occasion, they had been to a ball when George made some nasty comments about one of Caroline's relatives, who still danced, even though she was married. Caroline defended her relative until

"he suddenly sprang from the bed, siezed me by the nape of my neck and dashed me down on the floor. The sound of my fall woke my sister and my brother in law who slept in a room below and they ran up to the door. Mr Norton locked it and stood over me, declaring no one should enter. I could not speak, I only moaned. My brother in law burst the door open and carried me downstairs. I had a swelling on my head for many days after".

Caroline left George, but always returned for her children. The law at this time stated they belonged to him. She discovered this when becoming involved in an adultery scandal with Lord Melbourne. He was only a friend but   George   saw   it   otherwise.

"After the adultery trial was over, I learnt the law as to my children, that the right was with the father, that neither my innocence nor his guilt could altar it, that not even his giving them into the hands of a mistress would give me any claim to the custody. Mr Norton held my children as hostages, he felt that while he had them, he still had power over me that nothing could control"

It was while George was holding her children hostage that one of her sons died after falling off a horse. Caroline was sent for, but George had sent them to Scotland, by the time she got there it was too late.

Caroline fought back. She educated herself as to the law and began to write. Her pamphlet 'The Natural Claim of a Mother to the Custody of her Children as affected by the Common Law Rights of the Father' challenged discrimination against women and in 1839 the Custody of Children Act was passed by Parliament.

George was outraged by Caroline's writing and success. Lord Melbourne had also died and left her a small legacy, as had her mother. Legally though this money belonged to George. She refused to give it to him though and began another campaign. In 1854 she wrote "English Laws for Women in the 19th Century"

In 1857 the Marriage and Divorce Act was passed and though by now Caroline had found love, George refused to grant her a divorce. He maintained his control over her until he died in 1877. Only then was Caroline free to marry her new man. She was 69 years old and just a few months later, she too died.

1839 CUSTODY OF INFANTS ACT

This Act enabled a mother to apply to the court for the custody of her children up to the age of seven and for access to older ones

Meanwhile …

Michael Yates was charged with beating very brutally and threatening to murder his wife in 1841, near Abergavenny. As he could find no bail money for good behaviour towards 'her Majesty's subjects' and especially his wife he was sent to Usk House of Correction for six months.

In July 1843, George Gibbens, 27, was charged with the murder of his wife Charlotte by striking her and kicking her. They had not been married for very long and became unhappy so they separated. She found work as a tailoress but he continued to pursue her and became jealous when he thought she was with another man. It was while she went to a shop to buy some pins that Gibbens went in, swore at her, dragged her out into the street and hit and kicked her. She took to her bed after the attack for three weeks before dying. When examined it was found she was covered from head to feet in bruises. Gibbens was transported for ten years.

In Oxford in 1844, Edward Butler was tried for the murder of his wife by kicking her and beating her. The jury returned a verdict of manslaughter and transported him for life.

In January 1848 in Glasgow, George Fay was charged with culpable homicide and also the cruel, barbarous and unnatural treatment of his wife Margaret in so far as on 30th June 1847 he caused his wife to be confined in a water closet until 23rd September following which from the effects of such treatment, she died.

George Campbell, Inspector of the Poor, said

"I went to the prisoner's house on 23rd September. I inquired for the prisoner and found he was at home. Asked prisoner where his wife was. He said in the country and would be home the next day. Told him I must see her as I had information that she was in the house. There are three rooms, a kitchen and a water closet in the lobby. There was a window a foot square in the door of the water closet. I asked the servant, Margaret Hume to light a candle and asked the prisoner again if his wife was in the house, when he admitted she was. He was then leading me to a room behind when I noticed a bar across the water closet door, which fastened so that no one within could move it. I asked prisoner if she was there and he admitted that she was. I turned the bar and the door came open and I found her there. It was five o clock in the afternoon and we could not see without a candle. I found her lying with her body upon a sort of wooden bed, with her head on the seat of the water closet, and her body crouched towards the door. Her body was covered with a loose black covering, of a sort of cotton cloth; she had no shift or cap on and was in a state of nudity. She was lying in filth, with no bedding below her, and the straw was all wet. Her hair was matted like a door mat and the vermin were innumerable. From the way in which she was lying, her body had broken out a little. The straw apparently had not been removed from the time she went in, as it was all rotten. I measured the closet; the distance from the door to the back of the wall was four feet three inches; and the breadth of the closet was two feet ten and a half inches, but there were standards at each side of the door, which narrowed the breadth six inches. We lifted her out and set her on a chair but she could not sit up, her legs being drawn upwards towards her body. We removed her to the kitchen and set her in a chair with her feet on the fender to support her on the chair. I asked her name and age and how long she had been there. She stated that she had not been out but once since her incarceration in the month of May last. I desired the servant to bring her some clothing and she said that deceased had no clothing but she would bring some of her own. She did not bring any in my presence. I heard the prisoner say to his wife

"Sit up my dear"

But she seemed to think his kindness was mere show and paid no attention to it. Her eye was all putrified and a large lump of mortified matter upon it. Her nose was off her face. There was a very strong stench; so much so that I could hardly stand it and the officer with me had to leave the house. I asked the prisoner why he had kept her in such a place. He said she had been very disorderly and he had put her there in order that she should not disturb the neighbours. Prisoner said she was wrong in her mind. He said that she was very disorderly at times and that she was insane.

From the conversation I had with her I considered her in a sound state of mind. In defence, an attempt was made to show that the wretched woman was of unsound mind and of such disgusting habits that she polluted every place she came to; and that consequently it was necessary to confine her, though it was denied that she was never permitted to leave the water closet, but, on the contrary that she could come out when she liked". The jury however returned a verdict of guilty and the Lord Justice sentenced him to transportation for life

In 1853, David Murphy, described as of Herculean frame assaulted his wife Ellen. She was found insensible by the injuries he had inflicted. He had come home at midday, drunk and she hid under the bed from him. He took various items from the house, left and then returned for more. He did this several times when finally he went to bed. He realised she was under the bed when she coughed. He jumped out, pulled her out by her hair, jumped on her and kicked her. Six weeks prior she had delivered a stillborn child through his cruelty.

When asked, her husband said it was she who was abusing him. A surgeon certified that she was covered in bruises. He was remanded for a week until the extent of her injuries were ascertained.

In the Monmouthshire Merlin of 1853 an article on wife beating was published.

"Four ruffians in human shape were today brought up on separate charges, for violently beating and maltreating women.

Such a scene as was presented this morning, from the pale and frightfully haggard countenance of a wife nearly beaten to death, to the blood stained and disfigured face of an 'unfortunate' who had provoked a bully's jealousy, we have not witnessed during the last fifteen years in the Newport court.

Unhappily the practice of woman beating has become of frequent occurance. With the increase of magisterial power to punish ruffianism of this kind, under the new Act, it would appear that in various parts of the country a kind of mania for striking, kicking and half killing women has sprung into existence. As the Morning Chronicle justly observed a day or two ago -

'Women beating has decidedly become the popular amusement of the day. Drunkenness itself is it seems an imperfect state of enjoyment until the ferocity of our brutes has been heartily and thoroughly expended in kicks and cuffs on the first person whose sex, instead of protecting, marks her out as fair game for every species of cruelty … the police reports continue to furnish daily records of assaults on women; and the London journals are compelled day after day to reveal to the world that revolting habits which would disgrace the most degraded race prevail among gangs of wretches in this metropolis'"

Edward Leach was brought up on a charge of wife beating. His wife had a neck covered in contusions. They had been married for two years and he ill treated her daily. He never came home in the evening without doing so. After she got his breakfast one morning he asked her to give him some money. She replied she didnt have that much so he threatened to kick her brains out and commenced beating her around the head. He also grabbed her by the hair and bit her all over her body. Then he threatened to kick her liver out. Her face was disfigured from his cruelty. He was sentenced to six months hard labour.

What was to be done with all this wife beating? In the October 9th edition of Lloyds Weekly Newspaper in 1853, ran an article called 'Apes of Husbands'.

"We are heartily ashamed and profoundly humiliated by the details that pollute our police reports; and in our shame and abasement are prone to give ear to any remedy however strong and original that shall end the abomination. What is the man who beats his wife? What is he, it has been asked but a debased animal, a mere ape with speech? ... We would have the Home Office rent 2 or 4 or 6 cages and apes costume would be a most reforming punishment .. such cages to be placed in different parts of the grounds in which should be confined and exhibited the human creatures who had degraded themselves to the condition of apes by brutally outraging the gentleness and dignity of woman.... No violence towards husband apes, a sign Visitors are requested not to pelt or poke their sticks or umbrellas at the brute of a husband"

Needless to say, it didnt happen.

In December 1853 James Wright was charged with beating his wife Ann. He had hit her on the head and cut open her skull. He also hit her in the face. She called out for assistance and people came to help. In court it was revealed she had been married for three years and had been beaten for all that time. He had also threatened to murder her and said to the police once let go he would smash her brains out. He was sentenced to six months hard labour in Holloway.

James Crosby, 39 of Pye Street Westminster assaulted his wife and put her in the London Hospital. They were passing through Cottage Row and he told her to make haste. She replied she was going as fast as she could. He then hit her with his stick across her face and broke her nose. His sentence, six months hard labour.

In July 1854, Alexander Bains was described as an idle drunk. He barely worked at his own business of being a barber but lived off the money his wife earned in an oyster shop. One night a policeman on the beat heard a man thrashing a woman. He knocked the door and though she did not call out, he knew she was there. A detective later went around and apprehended her husband.

The detective said the woman's face was so disfigured by bruises he couldn't believe she was human. There were marks all over her body and she was covered in blood. She was in a raving state. Her brother spoke in court of her husband's idle state and the ill treatment of his sister. He said his sister was hard working, having to provide for four children and her husband's demands for money. Mr Bains, who was drunk in the dock was called a worthless degraded brute by the judge who imprisoned him for six months after which he had to find sureties to keep the peace.

George Rose, described as a rough, dirty ruffian was a labourer in a dock. He was in court for assaulting wife Anne. She appeared in court with two black eyes and a swollen face, her head was bruised and her features mutilated. She was weak from blood loss and half starved. She said George never provided enough food. His beating had caused her to miscarry and he had already been in court for failing to maintain the family. For that he was sent to prison for a month. He sometimes gave her a few pence which kept her and her five children in food for three or four days. He was in court again because he had come home drunk and thrown one child from one end of the room to the other. When confronting him he siezed her by the throat. She broke free, he then threw water over the child. He continued to beat her, telling her he was determined to hang for her, her time was up. He grabbed her by the hair, dragged her along the floor and jumped on her. She screamed out, blood running from her nose and mouth, eyes almost closed up and managed to get to a window. There she called out to some people below to save her child and she threw it into someones arms. George then lifted her up by her heels and threw her out of the window. She was caught by her landlord who witnessed the event. A policeman arrived and arrested George.

George did not deny the charges, he told his wife he had a mistress and that she had outlived his liking and he meant to kill her. He was imprisoned in the House of Correction with six months hard labour. The Judge said he was sorry he could not sentence him for longer.

In 1856 an article appeared in the Leeds Mercury. It asked what was to be done with men who beat their wives. At the time, prison with hard labour was the only option. The article asked whether this was really a punishment. While inside the man was fed and clothed while she starved or had to go to the workhouse. The life of the husband inside might be monotonous, engaged in uninteresting work however once they were out they left with no fear of returning. The current punishment was no deterrant. It went on to say that in 1854 and 1855 there had been 877 convictions under the Act for the punishment of aggravated assault on women (Criminal Procedure Act 1853) in the metropolitan police district alone. Having tried fines, short term prison, long term prison flogging was suggested. A Bill was being introduced by Mr Dillwyn in the House of Commons. The article understood the punishment was degrading but asked how a wife beater could be degraded having already placed himself on the 'lowest scale of humanity'.

Articles also appeared against flogging. The Daily News of 1856 wrote

"it has already been discovered that imprisonment tends to envenom the feelings of the husband against the luckless author of his incarceration"

It called for a more just and enlightened answer. Women in the upper and mid classes could claim a divorce on proving cruelty, let the poorer classes have the same.

Flogging for wife beating was rejected, the beatings continued.

In June 1856, Mrs Chapman applied for protection at court from her husband of 28 years. She said he had always been cruel and a drunk. She appeared with two black eyes, he did not appear at all. To avoid the execution, he stayed away from home. Eventually though he returned. On opening the front door for him, he punched her in the face, hit her down and kicked her. On trying to escape he ran into the arms of a policeman and was sentenced to three months in prison.

1857 MATRIMONIAL CAUSES ACT

Divorce courts were established, women had limited access to divorce. A husband if he wanted a divorce had to prove his wife's adultery. A wife, had to prove her husband's adultery, plus cruelty, incest or abandonement. Meanwhile ...

In April 1857, Alfred Crook, landlord of the Royal Oak, Bermondsey was charged with ill treating his wife, Maria. He had locked her in a room with no food. Her brother found out and came to protect her.

Maria stated she had been married for six years and had been ill treated for most of the time. In the last instance her husband had pulled her out of bed and beaten her. This had been witnessed by the barman who said he heard Mr Crook say he would 'do' for her, i.e, hang for killing her. Mr Crook appeared in court and blamed his bloated appearance on drink. He told the judge he did not care his wife had brought him there. He was sent to prison.

Education was the next suggestion to stamp out wife beating. An article was published in The Era of July 19 1857.

"If then we cannot benefit the existing race or lash them by correction or by precept into the guise of humanity or the responsible position of man, let us at least bend all our faculties to the rising generation and embody in our future scheme of National Education such a curriculum of instruction as shall make the moral duties and social obligations that unite man with society as much and imperatively a part of the peoples education as the ordinary class instruction of the school and let the foremost lesson taught be respect to women"

For   boys "teach him to know and appreciate the obligations that as infant and man and through all the phases of life he owes as a duty a love to woman; and in whatever sphere of life she may be placed it should become his pride as a man to acknowledge with love and recompense her with protection"

Thomas Elsbury obviously didnt read the article, he was in court in February 1858 for beating his wife and children. His wife had already left him but returned on his promise not to use violence again. She had gone to get his tea ready but noticed something displeased him. She asked him if he would like anything else. He said 'no' and sprang towards her. Their eldest daughter screamed for help but Thomas siezed her by the hair and swung her around the room. He then locked the door on his wife and tore hair from her head by the handful. Her screams led to a crowd gathering who broke down the door to rescue her. A policeman saw a mob of around two hundred when he arrived. Once inside the house he found Thomas brandishing a poker. His wife's hair lay around the room and the children had marks of violence. He was sentenced to three months hard labour.

In May 1858, as reported in The Era, the first case was tried in the new Matrimonial Court before Judge Sir C Cresswell. It was instituted by Mrs Tompkins who had been married for ten years. They had five children and she acted as a clerk to her husband's potato selling business, keeping the books etc. One year into the marriage he began hitting her with his fists on a daily basis. He also had a child by another woman, his wife knew of this because as treasurer she had to make the weekly payments to the other woman. She sought help after he threatened to hit her brains out with a poker. His defence was, it was for her own good as she kept accounts badly and he did make a point of sparing her face. The beating he said made her more docile and a better book keeper.

Mrs Harlow gave evidence against her husband in July 1859 She said

"On Monday night he dragged me down by the hair of the head and struck me with his fists til I was much injured and I think he would have killed me if I had not received assistance. He has frequently beat me most severely. On Saturday last he threw two chairs and a table at me and injured my eyes".

She expressed willingness to forgive him if he promised to behave himself. The magistrate counselled them to live happier lives in future. He liberated defendant on payment of the expenses.

Around 1860 a move by Lord Raynham to introduce his flogging Bill had its second reading in Parliament

"While corporal punishment still continues to be inflicted for comparitively slight offences in the army and navy, the most savage assaults upon women and children may be perpetrated by their natural protectors without fear of the lash …. Already police magistrates unanimously testify from experience how unwilling women in general are found, even under the present Act, to denounce their tyrants to the law. Sometimes affection, sometimes poverty, sometimes the dread of subsequent vengeance will make a woman suffer all extremities rather than inflict six months imprisonment on the man for whom she may feel a lingering tenderness, who may be the supporter of her and her children or whose evil passions she may be afraid of arousing into tenfold violence".

Lord Raynham lost by 226 votes to 86.

In August 1863, a Captain Francis Havilland had his views published in a newspaper, that a wife should

"have no desire but to make her husband happy ...what is more likely to destroy the comfort of a man on his return home from a day's toil than to see his children neglected and his wife dressed out in unbecoming finery with skirts expanded with crinoline and often under the influence of intoxicating drink, no comfortable meal awaiting his return, the house in disorder and the children crying for bread? It drives the man to the public house, it leads to quarrelling, wife beating and often to murder"

The laws may have changed but attitudes didn't, a woman's place was still to be in the kitchen, slaving away and if she didnt do as she was told it was ok to kill her.

On Christmas Eve 1864, Matthew Atkinson came home drunk from the pub and began to beat his wife with fire irons. He threatened to shoot anyone who entered the house and later informed neighbours he would kill her. No one stopped him. He carried on until she was dying. He then called neighbours and asked if they would help, they lifted her onto the bed where she died.

The police recorded the floor was covered with blood and hair as if she had been dragged about. A poker, tongs and coal rake were bent. A fire shovel had also been used, the blade covered in blood. He had also used the handle of a house brush and had broken it from the force of the impact.

The doctor described her body as a mass of bruises. It seems the house was rendered unhappy by his wife's habits. She had no money and was unable to provide supper for him. He had found kindness and severity had not reformed her so he knocked her teeth out and fractured her jaw.

The court learned Mr Atkinson had been out with some miners to a pigeon shooting match. He arrived so late home Mrs Atkinson had fallen asleep and had let the fire go low. Her nephew, who was also out with Atkinson, ran on ahead to warn her of his impending approach, knowing how nasty he was, but he couldn't wake her. When Atkinson did arrive, she was awake, she and her nephew ran, but Atkinson caught her, dragged her home and beat her. Then after the attack, while women attended to her body, he sat by the fireside with his miner friends and smoked.

He was convicted of murder but the newspaper that covered the story called for some kind of punishment for those that did nothing to help.

Maurice Hennesy, 27, was charged with beating his wife at Stepney Causeway in 1865. Her brother, aged 10 had attempted to save her and said 'Don't kill my sister". Hennesy siezed the boy, raised him above his head and threw him violently on the floor. An old man passing by, Mr Moody, intervened but he was also hit repeatedly causing his mouth and nose to bleed. Later, Hennesy siezed his wife by the throat and tried to strangle her, she then fled to her parents. He was sentenced to four months hard labour.

In 1866, James Marten was charged with beating his wife with a carter's whip. Four months hard labour.

Later that year, John Savage and his father, George were in court for cruel treatment towards John's wife Emma.

She had been married for four years and had one child. They lived in George's house and for three months her husband had not spoken to her. She was forced to live in a separate room with no chair or table meaning she had to sit on the floor. Her meals were sent to her door and she also had to sleep on the floor.

One day she went for a visit to her aunt and on return expected to see her supper waiting as usual, but there was nothing. She waited but on hearing her husband and father in law's bedroom doors shut, presumed they were going to bed. She went downstairs to where her husband was sleeping to ask if she could have some food. He told her no and that if she wanted some she would have to go to the workhouse for it. George then appeared and called her names. He threw her out of her husband's room but later relented when he realised she was hungry and went to get her something to eat. Her husband though, grabbed hold of her, shook her and hit her head against a wall. George intervened and told him he should not hit her anymore. She then went to her room and slept on the floor.

John's defence was that he had heart disease and excitement made his heart beat so fast he could not breathe properly. A doctor had said he had to be very quiet or he would die. He had married in the hope of a peaceful life but unfortunately his wife was an actress and had more money than he did. She also left him for long periods of time and was so ill he could barely get out of bed. He was bound over to keep the peace for six months.

One Tuesday night in January 1868, the son of Catherine Reilly arrived at his Gran's house, crying. He said to her.

"Oh Gran, my dada is beating my mama, I know she is dead"

The grandmother went to her daughter's house and found her on the floor in a pool of blood. She told her son in law to take Catherine to the hospital. His response was

"Take her where you like"

The Grandmother went to cover her daughter's body with a quilt but her son in law stopped her, so she took off her cloak and used that instead.

Her daughter was still alive but insensible. She put her into bed. Catherine called out 'mother' three times. The grandmother then left and went to get a police constable. On her return they found the children had been put into bed beside her. Catherine was then taken to hospital where she died.

Phillip Reilly, aged 11 was called as a witness. He stated that on the night he had been to a pantomime with his father and younger brother, Peter. After that they stopped at a pub and then returned home. Their mother had gone to hide from their father. She was under the bed. Their father pulled her out by her hair, beat her and kicked her in the ribs. She then went into a fit. Their father made the younger brother throw water over her. When out of the fit she called out for her mother. Their father then kicked her in the eye, kicked her in the back and ribs and threw her against the fire grate. Grabbing a candle he attempted to set her on fire but her clothes were too wet. He dragged her closer to the fire instead, putting her shoulders across the fender. Peter was at this point in bed, crying. Their father went to beat him. While attempting to do so, Phillip went to pull his mother out of the fire. Their father kicked her again and Phillip heard something in her crack. At that point he escaped and went to get his Gran.

At the trial, the father was emotionless. He had put the children into bed with Catherine to make out she was just sleeping. He was committed to be tried.

George Croft, married Mary Ann after one month. For the first fortnight they lived happily, then in July 1868 he became jealous. Mary Ann had made some purchases from a shop and when she gave her name as 'Miss', he became jealous and beat her. Soon after they went out to a dance and a man spoke to her. She knew him slightly. George asked her what the man was doing, dragged her into the street, put her in a cab, grabbed her throat until he nearly strangled her.

"Directly we got home" she told the court "he sent the servant out and then he began to beat me most disgracefully. I lay almost senseless on the floor (she began sobbing). I gave him no provocation at all. When the servant went back I went to bed. She interfered to protect me and he pushed her out of the room. I went upstairs and when I was undressed my husband came up with a pistol in his hand and he beat me unmercifully with a riding whip. I was naked. Next morning he accused me of kissing a gentleman then he began to beat me again with a horsewhip"

For George, it was urged that he had been provoked to strike Mary Ann because she had permitted improper familiarities to take place between her and the man and because she had been guilty of violent conduct at home. The magistrate after vainly trying to induce Mary Ann to settle the matter privately, fined George 40 shillings.

In 1868, Eliza Smith was nursing her daughter who had been confined for eleven days, when her son in law James Denyer came home drunk. He went up to his wife and threatened to beat her brains out. He struck her under the left breast and knocked her over a chair. She had not been provocative and had only asked him where he had been. He also threatened to hit Eliza because she interposed. His wife said 'you shall not hit my mother'. He then pushed her into a chair. He also beat her on her previous confinement. He was sent to prison for 21 days with hard labour.

In the House of Lords, Marquis Townshend moved the second reading of the Aggravated Assaults Amendment Bill in May 1869. The Trewmans Exeter Flying Post was

"happy to say the motion was lost. Its rejection is a thing upon which to congratulate not so much the wife beating husbands against whom the provisions of the Bill were in part directed as the unfortunate wives whom it was intended to protect. The measure proposed to confer upon the magistrates a summary power to order that a man should be flogged"

The paper also felt the law could be abused by malicious wives but also that upon prison ending, a husband could go back home and the whole cycle would begin again. Would flogging make him even angrier? What was needed was cruelty alone a sufficient ground for divorce.

Later that year, David Howell was charged with being drunk and riotous in Bridgend and beating his wife in the street. A policeman saw him. She had been complaining of the little money he brought home. As he had been drinking he hit her. The Bench told him it was well for him that they had only the charge of drunkenness and fined him five shillings.

Elijah Woodward went to his wife demanding money for drink. She refused and he knocked her down and kicked her in the eye. He had done no work for three years but lived on her earnings. He had assaulted her on two previous occasions but she did not prosecute. He alleged it was she who was the drunk and she fell and hit her eye. The policeman said she was sober and he was sentenced to three months in the House of Correction.

The law at this time still stated that what a woman earned belonged to the husband, that was about to change.

1870 MARRIED WOMENS PROPERTY ACT

A long running campaign led by women's groups led to this Act. Before this date, when a woman married she was required to give up all rights to anything she owned to her husband. Even items such as jewellery, she could not sell without his permission. But now, a woman's money was her own. Meanwhile...

John Mount Stevens was charged with assaulting his wife at Coed Y Gric, near Pontypool. At the suggestion of the magistrate, Mr Greenway, who appeared for the wife, endeavoured to effect a reconciliation without the case being gone in to. The husband however appeared to want to wash his dirty linen in public and would not consent. Mrs Stevens was sworn and deposed to habitual ill treatment and afraid he would do her some serious bodily harm. Mr Stevens said his wife had the temper of the devil but Mr Greenway retorted that going by the behaviour of Mr Stevens in court (which was of a very violent tempered man), it showed he had two or three devils inside him.

Mr Stevens was bound over in £10 to keep the peace for six months. He loudly declared justice had not been done and his wife, who had gone to her father's, should never live with him again! He also had to pay the 8 shillings and sixpence costs.

In Wolverhampton in March 1870 a miner named Patrick Jennings took the life of his wife Catherine. They were both about 40 years of age with six children. He was described as of a quarrelsome nature. He often beat his wife and she was known to have fits.

After a bout of illness that had lasted twenty weeks, he had resumed work and went with his wages to Wolverhampton market, with his wife.

They were known to have gone into several pubs and at midnight were making their way home. It was then he began to beat her and drag her along the road. On reaching a blacksmith's shop he dragged her to the rear of the building and continued to beat her using half a brick. He returned home at five in the morning where his children were sitting up waiting for them both to return. He said to his son, who was about 12 to

"come and help him home with his mother"

The two fetched her from behind the blacksmith's shop. The son said she stopped breathing just as they got her over the threshold. The children called for help from neighbours who found her dead, her face and body disfigured and bruised, the results of kicks. Shortly afterwards the husband admitted to killing her.

In the Wolverhampton police court he justified himself by saying he had

"a right to do as he liked with his own wife"

The police produced a broken brick clotted with blood. There was also much blood behind the blacksmith's shop. His defence was that he and his wife had drunk brandy and that it had overcome them and also when she drank she had fits. He was remanded.

William Potts was charged by a police constable with assaulting his wife in March 1872. The police constable said he saw him hit her and knock her down. Mrs Potts said she was drunk at the time and deserved all she got! He was still fined ten shillings and costs.

In May, a woman named Coates was walking along an incline near Llanelly when she saw a man named Brise carrying a sack. Looking more closely she observed legs protruding from the sack and realised he was carrying a dead body. She caught up with him and accused him of committing a murder. This he denied with an oath and pushed her away from him. He went on his way, but shortly after Mr Margraves, proprietor of a colliery, detained him and a search was instituted. Under a hedge they found a dead woman, bruised and discoloured about the body.

Brise was taken into custody and it appeared he had come home drunk and had beat his wife with his fists and a poker. A man named Rees called him a brute for ill treating his wife upon which Brise turned on him. Next morning Mr Rees saw Brise crying. He told him his wife had left he house and taken his money. Mr Rees tried to comfort him and told him his wife was sure to come back but he replied

"Oh no, she'll never come back to me again in this world"

He was charged with murder.

In the Mendip Hills, a man named William Lease in a fit of jealousy kicked his wife to death. He accused his wife of having been on the 'Hundred Acres' with a hundred men. Asking what he meant, he knocked her down. She had a baby in her arms at the time, who was taken away by one of the other children. The woman ran to the houses in the neighbourhood but did not receive any assistance. At the last house she went to for help, the door was locked against her. Her husband then dragged her to the garden and began beating her. While on the ground he kicked her on various parts of the body. He was then seen carrying buckets of water from a brook and flinging them over her. The neighbours at this time did nothing, it was said they even watched from their windows.

A man named Wood later went to Lease's house, where the wife's body was reclined in a chair. He admitted to killing her and said he was ready to answer for it. He was given into custody. The wife's body was covered in bruises. Three front teeth were knocked out, the upper lip and right ear were cut right through. There were numerous scalp wounds, one straight through to the bone. The body was almost naked, her clothes being torn up around the house. The floor was saturated with blood and water, the walls covered in gore.

A verdict of wilful murder was given, and those who knew Lease's wife said she was a well conducted woman and he should have had no suspicions about her chastity.

Also in 1872, the wife of John Moss appeared in court, her face bruised and eyes almost closed. He sent her out to get some tea and said she had been too long. He rushed at her and kicked her. Her body was also bruised. He had treated her violently on other occasions but she was reluctant to prosecute. He said he was sorry for what had occurred. The Judge said he was probably more sorry for the position he had placed himself in and sentenced him to six months hard labour.

In September of the same year, George Williams objected to his wife being out with a female friend. He knocked her down and kicked her. She had been married for seventeen years and did not wish to prosecute. Mr Williams had also got hold of her head and bumped it on a kerbstone and kicked her in the chest. After assaulting her he ran off. Another man was going to pursue him but got threatened by friends of Mr Williams. A surgeon examined Mrs Williams and reported bruises on her forehead, chest and a recent arm dislocation. He was sentenced to six months hard labour.

James Godwin, 27, pleaded guilty in May 1874 to the murder of his wife by beating her on the head with a portion of a bedstead. He was executed at Newgate prison. The cause of the crime was jealousy, she hadn't met him when she was supposed to.

Lloyds Weekly Newspaper ran an article in September 1874. It stated that the increase of crimes of brutal violence towards women was a 'terrible feature of English contemporary life … so common that lodgers who hear cries of women take no notice'.

It then detailed the case of John Bishop who had kicked his wife Mary Ann Ford to death. A doctor discovered a series of wounds over the left side of her head and from her forehead to the base of her skull. Her face was bruised as well as her arms and hands. There were also wounds on her chest and back and she had a number of ribs fractured, the bones had penetrated her lungs. She also had long and deep wounds on her legs. The blame was put on Gin!

In October 1874 the wife of Thomas Jones was reluctant to appear in court and denied he had hurt her but when pressed admitted he kicked her. The judge regretted he did not have the power of flogging and sentenced him to twenty one days in prison with hard labour.

James Smith was sentenced to three months in prison for his constant habit of beating and kicking his wife. One night he had arrived home drunk, kicked her, knocked her down, attempted to strangle her and beat her about the body.

At Dudley police court, still in 1874 Joseph Malloy was sent to prison for three months for kicking his wife and causing her to miscarry. He had also kicked three of her teeth down her throat.

In the County Observer and Monmouthshire Central Advertiser in November 1874 a parody of an air was published, to be sung to the tune of "The Beating of my own Heart"

The Beating Of My Own Wife

I'd melted all my wages
Ere of beer I had my fill
For a bob I asked the Missus
There's a way where there's a will.
She refused, I took the poker,
The neighbours never stirred
For the beating of my own wife
Was the only sound they heard.

A sneak blow to the Crushers
I was lugged afore the Beak
But I know'd that it was nothing
The old gal had her squeak
They fined me forty shillings
I paid it like a bird

And the beating of my own wife
Perhaps, that night was heard.

But rights is rights no longer
Cross swears he'll eat his hat
Or jolly dogs, as wops their gals
Shall suffer from the Cat.
If that brutal measure passes
Take William Sikes his word
That the beating of his own wife
Will not again be heard.
                    - Punch.

Prison sentences were appearing to have little effect. In June 1875 John McCamney left prison having served two months for assaulting his wife. He went home, kicked a cake of bread off a griddle on the fire and beat her up again. He was sentenced for another two months.

The wife of John Sharkey appeared in court in August 1876. Her face was covered in blood. She stated she had been married for twenty one years and he frequently assaulted her. She had been to meet him to ask him for some money. He replied he would not give her any but would give her two broken eyes. She said she would bring him to court but his reply was that he didnt care and he hit her on the temples and gave her two black eyes. She had supported him for five weeks when he had been ill and now he had recovered he refused to work. On previous occasions he had tried to stab her causing her to cut her fingers which were permanently bent and he had broken her ribs while in an advanced stage of pregnancy. He was sentenced to six months hard labour.

William Head appeared before court in November 1876. He had kicked his wife Mary Ann in the head with his boots. He had also been charged the previous year with kicking her so hard he knocked her eye out. He was then remanded for a week but she refused to charge him. The judge considered the case sufficiently proved though, and sentenced him to six months hard labour. For his current charge a police sergeant said he was more 'brute than man'. The judge regretted he could not be flogged but would prevent his barbarity by sentencing him to five years penal servitude.

In December 1877, John Landers was sent to prison for two months with hard labour for hitting his wife, Ellen, on the head with a poker.

1878 MATRIMONIAL CAUSES ACT

This Act of Parliament allowed women who were victims of violence within marriage to obtain separation orders. It could be obtained from a magistrates court, it wasnt quite a divorce, but it was available to working class women as it was much cheaper and gave them custody of children under ten. Meanwhile …

Richard Hotchins was committed for trial in May 1878 for attempting to murder his wife by beating her on the head with a jug, which broke causing terrible injuries.

The new law was reported on in the Aberystwyth Observer in June. The clause was added by Lord Penzance and as amended stated

"If a husband shall be convicted summarily or otherwise of an aggravated assault within the meaning of the 24 and 25 Vic. c. 106, sect 43, upon his wife, the court or magistrates before whom he shall be so convicted, may, if satisfied that the future state of the wife is in peril, order that the wife shall be no longer bound to cohabit with her husband and such order shall have the force and effect in all respects of a decree of judicial separation on the ground of cruelty and such order may further provide as to her support"

Francis Doyle was charged with three assaults on his wife Frances on 15th, 16th and 26th August 1878.

She was leaving the house when he caught her, tore her clothes off her shoulders and horsewhipped her. That evening she tried to leave the house, he beat and thumped her on the head, knocked her down and dragged her outside, through the gutter until her mouth was filled with mud. In the process he broke her wrist. She saw a doctor who sent her to bed for a week. Once the week was over, she attempted to see the doctor again to have her bandage tightened. Francis wouldn't let her go. She went back upstairs, he followed, kicked her in the back which made her run. Upstairs, he followed her and kicked her back down where he continued to beat her on the head. He was sent for trial.

James Barnsley was a police constable. He was formerly a soldier but his father had bought him out. He had entered the police force by means of using a false character. He had been married for three years and had committed frequent violent assaults upon his wife Sarah and had given her two black eyes. She worked while supporting him, he was described as a drunkard. In October 1878 he was given three months hard labour while his wife applied for a separation order. It was granted along with custody of the children and a maintenance order of six shillings a week.

In November 1878, James Stanton 27 was indicted for wounding his wife. Mrs Stanton left her husband on account of his cruelty and went to live with her father. Mr Stanton usually visited her on a Saturday night. On his last visit he had brought a pair of boots for their child but Mrs Stanton observed they were too big. In a rage he threw the boots on the fire. At one in he morning, Mrs Stanton's father told him it was time to leave. He then rushed upstairs, took the child out of the cot, siezed it by the legs, hung its head downwards and swung it violently back over his head. Mrs Stanton, horrified rushed to save her child but Mr Stanton hit her and ran out into the street. She followed and when she reached him he hit her again with a poker which he had grabbed on his way through the kitchen. She fell and then he dragged her by her hair for some distance. He then struck her on the head again with the poker and kicked her. As she lay on the ground he jumped on her, placing one foot on her face and the other on her breast. Her screams attracted attention and she was rescued and taken to hospital. The jury found the prisoner guilty of wounding. His Lordship told him they had taken a very merciful view of the case. He hoped the prisoner and those who heard him would fully understand that such outrages would be repressed by the infliction of the heaviest penalties prescribed by the law. He could not help but think that too much leniency was given to crimes of violence as compared with crimes against property but as long as he had the honour of a seat on the bench he would endeavour to repress these terrible outrages. He passed a sentence of 20 years penal servitude.

At Cardiff police court in 1879, Michael Driscoll was charged with beating his wife. He had returned home drunk and beaten her. He confined her to the house afterwards for several days but she managed to escape and ran to the police where she was examined and found to be covered in bruises. Her back, shoulders and arms were blue from being beaten with a stick. She had with her a baby, 14 days old and stated her husband had begun beating her not long after her confinement. He was sent to prison but only for a month because the bench considered he had been provoked by his wife liking to have a drink.

In St Lukes, Elizabeth Gibson the wife of a packing case maker died from the severe effects of a beating inflicted by her husband. He was arrested and charged with her murder.

Also in 1879, William Cassidy was charged with the attempted murder of his wife. He lived in Manchester with his five children. His wife was addicted to drink. In the early hours of a Sunday morning a police constable was passing and saw smoke issuing from a window of Cassidy's house. He obtained admittance and found in one of the rooms a bed on fire with a woman lying on it. He removed her to hospital. She was severely burned on one side, arms, and hands and later died. Before she died she stated she heard her husband going back downstairs when she awoke to find the bed on fire. He denied any knowledge of how the bed came to be alight. He was sentenced to death, however a petition was drawn up asking for further consideration to be given to the case as the petitioners declared the evidence inconclusive.

Domestic abuse wasnt all one sided, women could be the perpetrators too though stories about husband beating are much rarer, thats not to say it wasn't happening.

In January 1880, a Mrs Quairns murdered her husband by stabbing him in the breast with a carving knife. The pair were quarelling about a woman Mrs Quairns had brought to the house and her husband had ordered to leave. For some time the man defended himself with a tea tray against the onslaught of the wife but ultimately she managed to inflict a fatal wound.

In December of the same year James Faulkner was charged with the attempted murder of his wife. In the early hours of a Sunday morning while she was asleep, he struck her a heavy blow on the head with a hatchet. It cut halfway through the skull. Surprisingly, she didnt die and was able to return to her mother. He was committed to the assizes and declared he wished he had killed her.

John Kelly, at the age of 69 was sentenced to fifteen years penal servitude in February 1881 for the manslaughter of his wife by beating her on the head with a pair of iron tongs.

At Burnley police court, William Townley was charged with attempted wife murder. His wife had left him some months earlier due to his drinking habits. One day, as she was going about her work, he met her, followed her down the street and cut her throat with a pocket knife.

Still in 1881, Joseph Jarman, a travelling confectioner, argued with his wife in the Green Dragon Inn, Market Harborough. They had been separated for some time but she had agreed to meet him and offered to help him in his business. She refused however to live with him. Growing exasperated, he laid her head on the table and cut her throat. The woman was not expected to recover. Jarman was sent to the workhouse and stated her aggravating tongue had made him do it.

At the Leeds Assizes, James McGowan, a scavenger was indicted for the wilful murder of his wife on Christmas Eve. He and his wife lived in a small cellar in Keighley, she was employed as a rag picker. On Christmas Eve they went out together but became separated She was taken home, drunk, where he threw her into a corner in a heap. Through the night sounds of blows were heard and cries of 'murder'. He was prevented by a passer by from using a hammer. Next morning a neighbour went into the house and found the wife lying dead on the hearthstone. She had eighteen wounds on her head and face. He said he had beaten her because she had got drunk. He was sentenced to penal servitude for life.

Also at Leeds Assizes, Thomas Beckett was charged with the wilful murder of his wife Hannah on 15th December, She was accused of keeping improper intimacy with a man named Ogden and stayed with him as long as a week on one occasion and then returned home. On the day in question she told her husband she was going to meet Ogden which so enraged him that he cut her throat and attempted to take his own life. The jury found him guilty of manslaughter and sentenced him to four days imprisonment.

1882 WOMENS PROPERTY ACT

Allowed women to have absolute control over their own money and their own property. Meanwhile …

Elizabeth Jane Jones appeared at Newport County police court, her left eye severely bruised, the result of her husband's brutality. She stated she had been married to him for five years and had several children by him. He had ill treated her for most of their married life and on two occasions he had been sent to prison for it. He had kept her short of food and repeatedly threatened to kill her. He attempted to justify himself by saying his wife gave him 'cheek' and would not be silent. The wife's father asked the court to grant a separation as he was in no doubt murder would result if his daughter continued to live with her husband. The bench granted the separation and sentenced him to six months in prison with a maintenance order of 10 shillings a week.

In Birmingham in April 1882 a case was heard against a rope and twine maker named John Gill. The prisoner, under the influence of drink went home and without any provocation threw a heavy boot at his wife.   It struck her on the face. Afterwards he threw a parrafin lamp at her. Her clothing caught fire and, with a baby in her arms she rushed into the yard in flames. She called to her husband to give her assistance but he refused. She threw the child down and a passing stranger extinguished the flames. The woman was burnt over her body and her husband sent to prison for six months.

Timothy Sullivan of London, came home drunk one day in June. His wife implored him to give up drinking,. His response was to hit her across the head with an iron bar. He then ran away leaving her to die. He was later caught by the police.

In August the husband of Mary King had just been released from prison where he had been for four months after assaulting her. He got home and hit her several times in the face and threw a can of water over her. He said he was the 'devil out of hell' and would 'hang for her'. He did not attend court so a warrant was issued for his arrest.

James Bradley, described as a good for nothing idler, who lived off his wife's wages, met her one night as she was returning from work. Because she did not give him as much money as expected he kicked her along the passage that led to their cellar dwelling, where he abused her until she died. He was committed for trial on the charge of wilful murder.

In December 1882, Mr Price ws sentenced to six months in prison for brutally kicking and beating his wife. He had already completed a period of penal servitude for chopping off two of her fingers with a hatchet.

In March 1883 George Picklin of Birmingham made an attempt to murder his wife of two years. Owing to his constant cruelty she had left him and went to live with her mother. One morning she went to a neighbouring house to earn some money dressmaking and on returning to her mothers house found George there, who demanded money from her. She said she had none, that she had to support herself, her mother and two children. On receiving no money he produced a knife, threw her down and attempted to cut her throat. She cried 'murder' while trying to ward off the blade with her hands and with neighbours quickly appearing he was knocked down before he could finish his plan. The wife's hand was lacerated in a number of places. She was taken to hospital while he was arrested for attempted murder.

James Barton, fireman, was brought up before the county magistrate in Sunderland charged with murdering his wife. The woman's head was fractured in three or four places and her face was unrecognisable. She had been living apart from her husband and on the night of the murder he had been seen following her and making threats. He was arrested the following morning but when brought before the magistrate he had drunk a quantity of laudanum and had attempted to strangle himself in the cell, but was stopped by another prisoner. His wife was only 17.

At Manchester Assizes in July, Mary Morrison was charged with throwing sulphuric acid on her husband with intent to burn him. They were separated and he gave her a weekly allowance. She went to his place of work and asked him for some money. He said he would give her some when he drew his pension (as he was a pensioner). She took a jug from under her shawl and threw the acid into his face saying

"I will make you more blind than you are"

The man was injured though his eyesight remained intact. She was sentenced to five years penal servitude.

In Birmingham Thomas Clarke was remanded for a week for attempting to murder his wife. Immediately after his arrest the police were informed the wife had died from a blow to the head with an axe. It was supposed he was insane as he had been behaving in a very strange way, he was charged with wilful murder.

George Price, engine driver on the Great Western Railway was charged at Newport with assaulting his wife Mary Ann. Police Constable William Thomas said that he had heard a woman screaming 'murder' one Sunday night after midnight. He saw a man dragging a woman across the street. She told him she had been struck on the upper lip and on various parts of her body.. The man said his wife would not go home and had given her a severe blow. Her lip needed stitches. He was fined 40 shillings or a month's hard labour.

In December, 1883, Thomas Yates, a gun maker, escaped from the borough asylum near Birmingham by scaling the boundary wall. He made his way to a workshop he used to rent and took a bayonet. He then went to his former home and attacked his wife with the weapon inflicting serious wounds on her arm and a deep cut on her jaw severing the right artery. She was taken to hospital in a critical condition. Thomas had been in the asylum for six weeks and was believed to have recovered so much so he was considered harmless. He was remanded for a week to be medically examined.

A woman named Mrs Payne died in Derby Infirmary in August 1884. Her husband had thrown a lighted lamp at her which set her clothes on fire. At the time of the newspaper reporting the story, the man was not in custody.

In November in Clee, near Grimsby, Charles Briggs a chemist and his mother Elizabeth Briggs were indicted for the wilful murder by starvation of Thirza Briggs, his wife. The mother was acquitted while Charles got 20 years penal servitude.

A gardener named Mr Sannday from Cornwall, was charged with having adulterated his wife's soup with drugs, intending to do grievous bodily harm. The evidence of the nurse was to the effect that on two occasions the soup was discoloured and in one bowl white powder was found. She caught the husband before a stove while the soup was being prepared. Medical evidence showed the powder was calomel and a large dose. The husband was sent to the assizes.

1885 CRIMINAL LAW AMENDMENT ACT

For several decades, the Society for the Prevention of Cruelty to Children was concerned about the sexual exploitation of young girls. This Act raised the age of consent to 16 from 12 and brought about regulations to protect young women and girls from vice. Meanwhile ...

In Herefordshire, in January 1885, John Wright, aged 53 gave himself up to the police for the murder of his wife Eliza. He was brought to Leominster and remanded. John, a saw sharpener stated his wife came home and threatened to cut his eye out with a knife. He took the knife from her and having cut her throat, left the house. He returned at night and slept by the side of his wife's corpse and in the morning laid out the body. His home, an old turnpike house, on being visited presented little evidence of any struggle. The wife's body was found as he had described. The head had almost been severed from the body and the bed showed where he had slept beside her. Before the magistrates he admitted the crime

William Hopkins was charged with cruelty to his wife in Cardiff in August 1885. The woman stated that her husband had come home for his tea. Everything was ready for him but he was not satisfied. After some cross words between the pair he got a red hot poker out of the fire and drew it across her face. He then kicked her about the body. At the request of the Bench the wife was examined by a female at the police station who found various bruises on her body. The husband who had previously been convicted of violent assaults upon her was sent to prison for six months.

Daniel Minahan informed the police at Bromley-by-Bow that he had beaten his wife Bridget's head in with a hammer in a fit of temper. The woman was found at her house lying on the floor covered in blood with her head literally battered in. She was taken to hospital but died from her injuries. Minahan was arrested and charged with her murder.

In November 1885, William Harrison aged 30 was charged with attempting to murder his wife, Alice by hitting her on the head with a brick. Her mother heard her screams and saw her lying on the ground with him kneeling beside her. At the hospital Alice had suffered eleven scalp wounds, a bruised face and throat. He was remanded.

John Davies had been living apart from his wife Mary Ann for some years. She maintained herself and her son by cleaning and attending St Luke's School, Wolverhampton. She was engaged in her work when her husband entered the building, picked up a large poker and started to attack her. She tried to escape but he pursued her and hit her on the head. While she was on the ground he hit her again with the poker. The result was her skull was battered in and she died within a few minutes. Davies then walked out of the school and to the house of a police constable and gave himself up. After accompanying him back to the school, the officer saw the body and arrested him. He was charged with murder and replied

"I have had great provocation; she villified me too much. I have done the deed and I suppose I must suffer for it"

At the time of the murder a warrant was out for his arrest for using threats towards his wife. For some time she had lived in dread of him and was in the habit of locking herself in the school room when she went there to clean, out of fear her would get to her. Some of the teachers and school children were in the room when Davies began his attack but they were too terrified to interfere.

At Pontypridd police court, Howell Williams an aged man was brought up in custody charged with an assault on his wife Anne. She was also an old woman who the paper described from her appearance as 'not being an angel to live with'. She said that on Sunday morning she was in the act of lighting the fire when her husband got out of bed and requested she get him something to drink. She said there was some cold tea. He told her to go and get it. She went off to a bedroom but he followed her and hit her, making her nose bleed. He then said, 'Go and show that to them!' She screamed, he then grabbed her by the throat and throttled her saying 'I'll stop your windpipe' He threw her down and knelt on her chest. A lodger burst through the bedroom door and managed to rescue her. He found her on the floor under her husband who was beating her. Her mouth was covered in blood. She appeared exhausted and the lodger believed she would have died had he not intervened. He also stated the husband had a knife in his hand while beating her. He was sentenced to fourteen days with hard labour.

Charles Hodson, was tried at Liverpool for throwing vitriol on his wife, a chorus singer at the Prince of Wales Theatre. Hodson intercepted several letters including one signed 'Harry' and traced his wife to the Royal Hotel and other places. Prompted by jealousy he threw vitriol on her face outside the theatre and she was permanently disfigured. He piteously appealed to the jury, for his wife's heartlessness had driven him mad and he was not accountable for his actions. The jury recommended him to mercy and sentenced him to five years penal servitude.

A farmer, Patrick Nolan who had completed his prison sentence of five years was released. He returned to his home and murdered his wife with a spade. It was supposed his mind was affected by imprisonment. No trace of him was found to arrest him.

A labourer named William Wilkins was arrested by Sheffield police having made a murderous attack on his wife. They had been living apart for some time due to his violent nature. It was said that when he was in prison for assaulting her, he attempted suicide. On the day in question he sent his daughter to his wife's lodgings and requested to see her. She came out, and two minutes later neighbours heard her screaming. They found her on the ground with her husband kneeling on her, hitting her head with a brick.

1886 MARRIED WOMEN DESERTION ACT

A wife could apply to a magistrates court for a separation and maintenance order where there was wilful neglect to provide maintenance from her husband who was legally liable to maintain. Meanwhile ...

In August 1886 the people, of High Street, Tredegar were thrown into a state of consternation by hearing loud cries of 'murder'. The cries came from the house of John Watkins and on people arriving there found him beating his wife on the head with a steel bar and kicking her. The police at once took him into custody, The wounds on the woman's head were bound up and it was thought she would make a full recovery.

Hugh Daly a farmer living near County Armagh murdered his wife by kicking her in such a ferocious manner that her head was almost smashed to pieces. He then walked to town and surrendered to the police.

At Jarrow on Tyne, Michael Kirkwood murdered his wife. The woman had separated from him on account of his cruelty and went to live with her mother. Kirkwood met her in the street and hit her so hard with his fist he killed her on the spot. He was arrested.

The wife of Dudley Smythe appeared in court in May 1886. He though had absconded. They had been married for twelve years. The previous Christmas she had had words with him about a child by a previous marriage. She went to bed, he followed, hit her in the face causing her nose to bleed, he beat her several times, grabbed her hair, threw items at her and also threatened to murder her. The court considered the assaults not of so aggravated a character to order separation and he was fined 20 shillings.

In 1887, Charles Smith was a travelling tinker. In February he and his family pitched a tent made of blankets on Oxford common. Around five in the morning the children alerted people in a neighbouring cottage that their father had killed their mother. Two men went to the tent and found the woman dead, her head having been battered in. When the police arrived, Smith said

"Good morning, I have got a dead 'un this morning; my wife is dead"

He was brought before the magistrates that afternoon and charged with wilful murder of his wife Lucy.

In March 1887, the brother of Emma Douthwaite, 34, informed the police of his sister's ill treatment. He didnt go to see her himself as he was frightened of her husband's violence.

Emma's daughter, Mary Agnes, aged 10, said her father was drunk and had complained about her mother showing a man around an empty house. He kicked her in the stomach and back, hit her on the ear with his fist. A midwife had to be called who found Emma suffering a miscarriage. She later died.

The surgeon who examined her said she had a bruised lower abdomen, right eye and left ear were injured. Her chest and arm were bruised and all wounds a few days old. The verdict against the husband was wilful murder.

John White ran a shoemaking business with his wife Emily. They had been married for forty years. One day in 1888 she went out to deliver some work for her husband. She was paid 12 shillings. On her way home she stopped in the pub and once she did get home continued having a drink with her husband. When he asked her for some money she said she didn't have any, but subsequently gave him some. He picked up the poker from the fire and hit her several times on the head. He then went to a neighbour to ask for help in putting his wife to bed. He said to the court she had irritated him but he didnt believe he had caused injury. When asked if he would like to say anything he replied

"Yes I should like to say a few words. I never intended to hurt her; and if she had let me lie down for twenty minutes as I wanted I should not have hurt a hair of her head"

The judge sentenced him to death.

Also in 1888, Robert Bright, 29, was charged with wounding with intent to murder. He had beaten his wife Maria on the head with a plasterers hammer. There was no evidence as to why he had done it but her skull was fractured in two places. He absconded but was found at his mother's house and remanded.

Michael Coughlin had arrived home drunk in April 1889 and had had words with his wife. He then hit her on the shoulders while following her around the house. Evidence was given by their daughter who said she and her mother feared for their lives as he made threats to blow their brains out with his revolver. His defence was provocation. He was fined 40 shillings but a judicial separation order was refused.

Edward Henry Barton, a curate, was found guilty of assault in July 1889 but claimed he had been provoked by his wife using foul language – the word 'damned'. He had had a discussion with his wife Rachel Ann over one of the children. He asked why the devil she had not given the child some cough mixture? She said it was because it had not been required. He proceeded to hit her on the chest and against a wall several times, hitting her jaw. He was fined £2 and costs.

William Whitely attempted to murder his wife in November 1890 by hitting her with his fists. She had been confined six weeks before. He rushed to the bedroom in an attempt to murder the children but was stopped by neighbours. His wife said he had been restless all night and told her he had to kill her. She said he had always been good to her and the children previously though her face was barely recognisable.

He said in his defence

"It's been the visitation of God, it's been the curse of my life"

He remained unconcerned throughout the trial and was pronounced insane.

In March 1891, John Shaughnessy was charged with neglecting to maintain his family and had not done so for a long time. His wife and two children were removed to the workhouse in a starving state. The wife was dying from consumption. Not only had he left her and the children to live in destitution, he had also beaten her. The Bench sentenced him to three months hard labour.

The following month, one Saturday afternoon Edward Watts, 38 who was separated from his wife, went to the house she was staying at with her parents near Portsmouth. There he tried to persuade her to resume living with him. Failing to do so he took out a six chambered revolver and shot her. She was hit in the head, throat, right breast and was killed instantly. She was 34 and had several children.

David Kane of Edinburgh was charged with having murdered his wife in 1892, with a hatchet. It was alleged he was in the habit of drinking and they were frequently arguing. The wife on one occasion leapt out of a window to escape his violence.

At Barry Dock, Mary Logan was charged with violently assaulting her husband. It was stated by Dr Treharne that the husband was in a very critical condition and would be unable to leave the house for some time.

Mary appeared in the dock with a baby in her arms and cried bitterly. She was remanded for a week.

Martin King, a collier of Haydock near St Helens was remanded in October 1893 on a charge of wife murder. He and his wife had been walking home late at night and on reaching a lonely part of the road, he pushed her over a fence into a field. Despite her struggle he dragged her to a ditch, drew a large dagger from his pocket and plunged it into her neck below her right ear. Her cries attracted some men who were passing. Her husband fled leaving her in the ditch. He was caught a few days later, the crime was attributed to jealousy.

Benjamin Poneton, 30, was convicted of attempting to murder his wife. He locked her in the kitchen and attacked her with a hatchet inflicting many serious injuries. He afterwards cut his own throat and then re attacked his wife but a neighbour prevented any further injury. He told the doctor who attended it was due to jealousy. He was ordered to be detained at her Majesty's pleasure.

At midnight , one Saturday in August 1894, a wife murder took place in Oldham. Job Whitehead was separated from his wife and had been for about three weeks. He met her, on her return to her brother's house and putting one arm around her neck, with his right hand cut her throat with a razor, almost severing her head from her body. He then made a feeble attempt at cutting his own throat but was stopped by a passer by. So he ran off to a nearby reservoir and jumped in. He failed again in his purpose so got out and went home. A police sergeant went to Job's home and in reply to the sergeant's questions said

"Yes I tried to cut my throat and then tried to drown myself but I could not manage it"

He was cautioned and charged with the wilful murder of his wife upon which he asked

"Is she dead?"

On receiving a positive reply he then observed

"This all through a gay life"

Mrs Simpkins had been married for twelve months. She met her husband one evening in 1895, when for no reason he hit her in the face. Once home he ran after her with a cane but was stopped by a police constable. He told the constable he would 'do' for her. He was bound over to keep the peace.

In the opening month of 1896, the Rhyl Record and Advertiser ran an article regarding the new Acts. It stated that the number of ladies applying to Mr Paul Taylor at the North London police court was remarkable. Mr Romaine had made an application on behalf of one woman who said her husband had left her and showed no sign of returning. The summons was granted but Mr Taylor added that there appeared to be a mistaken opinion as to how far magistrates could go under the new Act. With regard to desertion the law was the same but a little more elastic with regard to cruelty and neglect. Another woman applied for a separation order because of her husband's bad conduct but Mr Taylor said she could not have a summons because persistent neglect had not been alleged and she was still living with him. However he said he would send a constable round to tell him to behave himself. After hearing several applications of a similar nature, Mr Taylor said he should not encourage wholesale summonses under the new Act and he would not take responsibility of advising wives to leave their husbands and to have the assistance of the New Act it must be proved to the satisfaction of the magistrate that wives had been obliged to leave their husbands because of persistent cruelty and neglect to maintain.

In May 1896, Mrs Noonan appeared in court, her face greatly disfigured. Her husband had ill treated her for their two years of marriage. They were about to have tea one day when without any provocation he kicked her on the nose with his heavy boot. He said she had provoked him for two years and that she had pawned his possessions.

The judge said that for such men he had one sentence, six months hard labour.

Mrs Noonan though began crying and appealed to the judge about what she was going to do. The judge's reply was that the court could not help her.

A few weeks later Charles Day was in court for hitting his wife on the head with a frying pan because she had been out all day. He got six weeks hard labour.

In 1895, William Morgan of Greenwich was charged on remand with the murder of his wife. Evidence showed that he waylaid his wife, from whom he was separated and after an argument, forced her onto her knees and stabbed her in the neck. He said to her during the assault

"I said I would do it if you followed me about"

John O Neill, of Cardiff appeared before the police court, as he had done many times previously, accused of assaulting his wife, Mary Ann by kicking her. He was sent to prison for six weeks with hard labour.

At Brentford police court in May 1896, John Bridgeman, described as a barge builder was charged with assaulting his wife. She appeared in the dock looking very frail with her arm bound to her side. She had been granted £2 from the poor box on account of her destitute condition. She stated that about two weeks earlier she had asked her husband for some money to get some bread for the children of whom there were four. He refused and on her asking a second time he hit her several times and knocked her to the ground. He then siezed her by her hair and 'banged her on the ground'.Grabbing a kitchen broom he struck her several times breaking her collar bone and a bone in her shoulder. She had the bones set by a doctor. A few days later he hit her again and told her to go to the hospital, when she would not do so he threw her to the ground and said

"I'll do for you when I get the opportunity"

The doctor said very great violence must have been used to cause such an injury and she must have suffered great pain.

The husband admitted the offences but said

"My wife made me wild because she would not go to the hospital and I threw her to the ground and broke her shoulder again"

He was sent to prison for four months, she was granted a separation order with a maintenance allowance of 15 shillings a week.

William Brown was charged with a violent assault, at Worship Street police court, London. His wife appeared in the witness box with a contusion of the eye. She said her husband would not work and was drunk. They had had an argument and he struck her in the eye with his fist. Ten minutes later he kicked her in the leg. She had previously suffered in the same way. A police constable went to the house and found the woman bleeding while the husband said that she had hit him first. The constable added a doctor was sent for and said the woman was so bruised she had been used more like a football than a human being. The judge said

"For treating your wife like a football you will go to prison for six months hard labour The wife can get a separation when you get out"

James Wimpney was charged with assault in 1897. He was drunk and had been calling his wife names. She told him to go back to the other woman he was seeing. He then took a poker from the fire and threatened to knock her brain out. He hit her on the back and arms and she fled to a policeman. The constable reported Wimpney fled downstairs and said it was not half of what she deserved. He was given six weeks hard labour.

Mary Flynn appeared in court with a black eye and a bruised nose. She also stated her husband Patrick assaulted their children. She had pawned her shawl and a blanket to get him some bacon and eggs. His response was to assault her. A police constable went to get him. Patrick said he might as well be in prison and the injuries given to his wife were by her sister in law. He was sent to prison for three months.

Edward Ratcliffe, an English actor popular with female theatre goers was in a New York court in December 1897 charged with cruelty and other indignities towards his wife who had applied for a divorce. During the trial, Judge Newberger said "wife beating might be approved of in some countries but not in America".

He hoped a severe sentence would be a warning.

The issue of flogging was raised again in 1898. A resolution in favour of judges having power to inflict flogging on men convicted of outrages on women and children was passed at the York Assizes by the Grand Jury. Mr Justice Darling said he would forward the presentation to the proper quarter, the Home Office. Many similar presentations had been forwarded to the same destination but the laws had not been altered. He had not encouraged such presentations, not because he disapproved of them but because he had no taste for 'piping to those who would not dance, or encouraging others to go through so futile a performance'.

"It was," he said "undoubted that if these crimes continued in the same proportion that they now held, with regard to assize calendars, there must be such a revulsion against those who committed them as would ensure some statute being passed as the Grand Jury had suggested".

In October 1898, as reported in the Evening Express, Dr Parker gave an address to a crowded congregation at the City Temple, London. He referred to the 'awful amount of wife beating prevalent throughout the country' and said that there was nothing more despicable than for a man to thrash his wife. If he (the preacher) was rich enough he would employ a band of men to thrash and give wife beaters - cowards that they were – an idea of their cruelty. Several persons had been trying to get a petition largely signed against flogging because it demoralised the subjects but what, he asked, could be more demoralising than wife beating?

The same month a man named William Slade shot his wife in bed. Mrs Slade, it was said, led a 'loose life' in Cardiff until she married. They then moved to London. What kind of life they led was difficult for the newspaper report to ascertain but it must have been unhappy as she left Slade and returned to Cardiff. One day, she attempted to find a room for her and her husband and found one at a house accommodated by a friend of hers. That night all seemed to go well, then on retiring to bed, the landlady heard two shots being fired. The police were called and found Mr and Mrs Slade lying on the bed, both had gunshot wounds to the head. A bullet had entered Mrs Slade's head at the right temple and a portion of her brain was protruding. She died about half an hour later. Mr Slade had shot himself in the face but he was not as badly injured.

It was surmised the motive of the crime was jealousy, the husband believing she had returned to Cardiff to resume her old way of life.

The fight against wife beating took a giant step backwards in April 1899 after a statement from Judge Peabody in a St Louis police court. He claimed that under certain conditions a husband had the right to beat his wife. Overseeing a case of a man who beat his wife because she would not agree with him in the management of their children, Judge Peabody said

"In this case, the wife was more guilty than the husband for trying to contradict and thwart her husband's will in the presence of the children and setting them a bad example which he had a right to rebuke. There are times when a wife irritates her husband to such an extent he cannot control himself and uses his hand or fist. As long as no serious harm is done I dont believe in punishment"

In July, in Dundalk a Mrs Crilly was found battered to death. She and her husband had had frequent arguments and she was addicted to drink. These arguments were renewed on the return of Mr Crilly from work and upon the door to the house being forced open by a relative who heard Mrs Crilly's shrieks, found her dead, battered with a heavy stick beyond all recognition. Mr Crilly was arrested.

The county police of Old Trafford, Manchester arrested John Percy Thompson on suspicion of murdering his wife Catherine by shooting her in the back of the head with a revolver. It was said they had lived unhappily together owing to his jealousy. They went to bed at midnight after an argument and two hours later a female lodger heard a loud bumping noise on the floor. Thompson asked her to go for a doctor and on his arrival the woman was found lying dead with a gun beside her. Mr Thompson was arrested and appeared unconcerned.

In Sheffield an inquest was held on the body of Ellen Holroyd, 44, who had died as a result of the injuries inflicted by her husband. He went home and found her drunk , so, in his own words 'banged her head against the wall' She died a quarter of an hour later. A verdict of manslaughter was returned.

John Henry Symonds was charged with cutting and wounding his wife in Cardiff. She appeared with her head and face bandaged. She said the wounds were inflicted during breakfast one morning when he attacked her without provocation with a razor saying he would give 'rest;' to both her and himself. Police Constable Hawkins said he arrested the husband who said

"If only you knew what I have been through lately it would make you or any other man do it"

He was sent for trial.

In Wolverhampton George Parker was committed for trial for attempting to murder his wife. He had not done any work for some years but lived off his wife's private income. After an argument, she left him but returned to their home later to remove furniture, her property, when he fired two shots at her. Fortunately for her, he missed.

Into the 20th century and David Craig was charged with assaulting his wife in June 1900. She had been beaten on her arm with a pickaxe. He denied it and said another man had done it with a knife. He was fined 20 shillings.

James McDonald of Newport ate his dinner and threw the empty plate through the window at his wife who went to sit on the window sill to escape his tantrum. Then he grabbed her by the hair, punched her in the face and kicked her. The wife, with a six month old baby said the trouble was all about his sister and the husband said he had reason to beat her as she pawned everything in the house. He was sentenced to a month in prison.

William Irwin was executed at Newgate for the murder of his wife on June 22nd. He was out of work and supported by his wife. One night, when she had no money to give him he told her

"You shall not live. You have driven the last nail in your coffin"

On the following morning he tried again to take money from her but failed as she had none and so he stabbed her with a knife. Irwin it was said, lived happily with his wife until the parties made friends with a man employed at Chelsea Hospital. Jealousy appears to have been the motive for the crime. As a result, Irwin was recommended for mercy on the grounds of provocation even though there appears to have been no cause for his jealousy. The Home Secretary though declined to interfere with the sentence and he was hanged.

Charles Plewitt was executed at Leeds for the murder of his wife. She was found with her throat cut sitting in a rocking chair while her husband disappeared. In Halifax, someone showed him a newspaper report of the murder alongside a portrait of himself but he showed no interest. On the first trial the jury disagreed but after the second hearing he was found guilty and sentenced to be hanged. It was said he was callous and indifferent to the last.

At Stafford Prison in April 1901 Joseph Shufflebotham was executed for the murder of his wife at Biddulph Moor. He broke into the house where she was staying, presumably they were separated, and cut her throat with a knife. He stated that she first attacked him after which he had no recollection of what happened though later in prison he admitted he had used a razor. He was found guilty of murder and condemned to death.

Patrick M'Kenna was executed in Strangeways Prison, Manchester for the murder of his wife at Bolton. He was jealous of her, frequently arguing with her. He accused her of misconduct with a lodger and, while drunk, stabbed her in the neck with a knife. She died soon afterwards. The defence was that there was insanity in M'kenna's family and that when in drink he was mad.

A petition for the remission of the death sentence was signed by thousands of Bolton people but the Home Secretary declined to interfere and so the death sentence of hanging was carried out.

William Kirk was sentenced to death at Lincoln for the murder of his wife Ellen. She had gone to nurse a sick neighbour and her husband became insanely jealous of Mr Robinson, the neighbour's husband. As a result he frequently went to the house and argued with his wife. He followed her into an outhouse and severed her head from her body. He then attacked Mr Robinson who managed to defend himself with a pitchfork.

In Northampton, Alick Claydon was executed for the murder of his wife. After a drinking bout, he got up in the middle of the night, battered his wife's head in with a shoemakers file, fractured her arm and stabbed her in the neck and heart. Next morning he went downstairs to cook himself some breakfast, which he then ate and returned to bed. Later he walked out into the countryside and gave himself up to the police The defence at his trial was he was insane.

In the Daily Mail of December 1901 was an article entitled "Rights of Man do not include Wife Beating". It concerned police in Birmingham who had heard cries from a house. Inside they found blood all over the place. The mother of the owner of the house smashed a plate over one of the police constables head and her son when in court asked what right the police had to enter his house as he had been 'chastising his wife'.

"Have I no right to chastise my wife?" he asked

"No you have not" replied the judge.

He said he was doing so because she was drunk.

The Victorians were at their wits end in trying to eradicate wife beating. The accounts in this book are just the tip of the iceberg, for every one that made the news there were who knows how many that went unnoticed. The Victorians thought up many punishments and introduced new laws but still domestic violence carried on and it still does. The final word goes to Judge Plowden, who in September 1904 when sentencing omnibus driver John Wilson to three months in prison for a brutal assault on his wife, said

"Week after week, husbands are brought before me for assaulting their wives and yet they will not learn that to assault women is against the law and against humanity"

20TH CENTURY

On January 1st 1900 women would have to wait

18 years before the Representation of the People Act, allowing women over 30 to vote.

23 years before there was equal divorce criteria between men and women.

25 years for the Guardianship of Infants Act, mothers were given equality in the custody of children.

28 years for the amendment to the Representation of the People Act which allowed everyone over 21 to vote

33 years for the marriage bar to be removed, in London

44 years for the Education Act which stated women could not be sacked upon marriage

46 years for the marriage bar to be removed for female civil servants

69 years for divorce to be granted on the ground of irretrievable breakdown.

70 years for the Equal Pay Act

75 years for the Sex Discrimination Act to become law.

75 years for the Employment Protection Act which made it illegal to

dismiss someone on the grounds of pregnancy.

76 years for the Domestic Violence Protection Act

91 years for marital rape to become illegal

REFERENCES

Liverpool Mercury
Hampshire Telegraph and Sussex Chronicle
Western Mail
Trewmans Exeter Flying Post
Birmingham Daily Post
Belfast Newsletter
Daily News
Lloyds Weekly Newspaper
Sunday Times
Newcastle Courant
Aberdeen Weekly Journal
The Times
Freemans Journal
Reynolds Newspaper
Bristol Mercury
Daily Mail
Monmouthshire   Merlin

ABOUT THE AUTHOR

Carol Ann Lewis was born in South Wales in 1969. She began writing in school and has had a number of poems published in anthologies. She has also written local history articles for a Cwmbran newsletter and contributed to local history publications by Cwmbran Writers Group. She is currently studying history with the University of South Wales. She has four children and six grandchildren

www.ingramcontent.com/pod-product-compliance
Lightning Source LLC
Chambersburg PA
CBHW070827290526
45795CB00002B/853